THE LI
FR
TIPS

WILLIAM FORTT

THE LITTLE BOOK OF FRUGAL TIPS

WILLIAM FORTT

Absolute Press

First published in Great Britain in 2011 by
Absolute Press
Scarborough House, 29 James Street West
Bath BA1 2BT, England
Phone 44 (0) 1225 316013 **Fax** 44 (0) 1225 445836
E-mail info@absolutepress.co.uk
Web www.absolutepress.co.uk

A catalogue record of this book is available from the British Library

ISBN 13: 9781906650254

Printed and bound in Malta on behalf of Latitude Press

‘Men do not realize how great
an income thrift is’

Cicero (106–43BC), Roman orator, philosopher amd politician

1

Thrift can be positive, if you look at it from the right end.

It's about independence, originality, inventiveness and simplicity, rather than mere tight-fistedness. Treat frugality as a challenge not a chore – and it'll be fun as well.

2

Use everything and waste nothing.

Before you throw something out, or pass it by, stop and think – can I find another use for it? Many objects and materials can be recycled at home. It's just a question of using your imagination to find new jobs for them.

3

Plan ahead and your money will go further.

It's easy to waste funds on things (or quantities of things) you don't really need. So set yourself a budget for shopping and stick to it like a limpet – no matter how many BOGOFs are dangled before you.

4

Go to markets other than supermarkets.

There are traditional weekday markets, farmers' markets and WI markets, not to mention farm shops, weekly box schemes and jumble sales. Here you are likely to get cheaper, fresher and more locally produced food than in the hallowed halls of the chain stores.

5

Buy dried food.

Rice, beans, lentils and other pulses are extremely nutritious, and make an economical substitute for meat (though they do demand a bit of imagination in the cooking). If you can find a shop where it's possible to buy loose dried food, you'll save even more money.

6

You can make stock out of almost anything edible.

Bung your (clean) vegetable offcuts into a pan, cover with water, and boil up with a few herbs. For fish stock, add skins, shells, heads and bones. For meat stock, add skin, bones and giblets. The result can be used as a base for soups and sauces.

7

Get the most out of your chicken.

Depending on size, it should do for at least three meals. First, hot from the oven; second, cold in a salad or in some moisturising sauce; third, in a soup made from the chicken stock. Give any remaining scraps of meat (with bones removed) to the dog.

8

Gather free food from the wild.

Go foraging in season (with a reliable identification guide). In spring, look for young nettles, ramson leaves and dandelions. In early summer, it's wild strawberries. In late summer and autumn, you'll find blackberries, crab apples, sloes and fungi of all kinds. There's plenty more, too.

9

Get yourself a steamer.

That way you can cook two or more dishes for the price of one. Steam speedy food such as couscous, lentils, vegetables and even small fish over something which has to simmer for longer (potatoes, meat casseroles, or dried beans). There's a bonus: they will pick up flavours from each other.

10

Make your own bread.

It's much easier and less time-consuming than you'd believe, and much healthier to eat. And, of course, your bread comes miles cheaper than the puffed-up shop-bought stuff. It works out at very roughly 80p a loaf – all for about 20 minutes of active preparation and kneading time.

11

Be choosy about the meat and fish you buy.

Fillet steak and dressed lobster are always going to be horrendously expensive. So look for cheaper cuts. Shin of beef, chicken wings and pork belly need more imaginative treatment, but are in many ways tastier. Same goes for mackerel, sardines, squid and grey mullet.

12

Take a packed lunch to work.

You can feed more cheaply, and probably more pleasantly and healthily, on food you've prepared at home than on shop-bought pasties and bacon butties from the office machine. Again: plan ahead. Make more supper so you can take the leftovers to work next day.

13

Join a local natural foods co-operative.

Co-ops are not out to make vast corporate profits, and can supply you with good (and usually organic) basic foods at a low cost. You may need to band together with a few friends to reach the minimum order levels and then share out the delivery.

14

‘Eat less’

may sound like a command for dieters,
but it’s also a reminder to

spend less

on food by ensuring that you

waste less.

Apparently UK householders chuck away 7 million slices of bread each day – and that’s just a start. Simply plan to serve smaller portions of food and drink. You won’t miss it.

15

Eat fruit and vegetables in season.

It stands to reason that fresh strawberries are going to be cheapest in June and most expensive in January. The same principle applies to asparagus, mushrooms, tomatoes and a hundred other things. Buy produce when it's plentiful and costs least.

16

Convenience costs money – that's why convenience foods are more expensive. So:

stick to unprocessed food as far as possible.

That means avoiding tinned beans, frozen pizzas and pre-cooked rice, and making your own. You do the preparation and processing – you keep the change.

17

Save money on cheese without sacrificing quality.

Look for cheaper varieties which you can substitute for more expensive and trendy ones – Stilton instead of Roquefort, Wensleydale instead of feta, pecorino instead of Parmesan.

18

Use brown rice and wholewheat pasta

instead of the refined versions.

They are economical (because they fill you up quicker and so you eat less), and very good for the bowels (because they have more fibre in them). They also taste intriguingly different.

19

Cook a meal in one pot

and save energy and time. Pop potatoes and other vegetables into your casserole fifteen minutes before serving. Roast vegetables in the same pan as your leg of lamb. Then there's risotto – the classic one-pot dish.

20

Grow your own fruit and vegetables.

Even a windowsill can produce a few herbs and cress. Bigger indoor spaces open up bigger possibilities (tomatoes, peppers, lettuces), and of course a garden is even better. Failing that, look around for an allotment to rent.

21

Plants need moisture to thrive, but it need not be fresh. **Collect rainwater or divert bath and other waste water** (within limits of course) into rainbarrels or any suitable large container. Let it settle for a time, then use it to water the garden in spring and summer.

22

Make the most of your vegetable seeds.

Seeds can be expensive, so start by sowing them sparingly (the seedlings will get away quicker this way). Then wrap up the remainder and keep till next season – somewhere cool and dry, or in a screwtop jar in the fridge.

23

Sow salad seeds in modules

(trays with individual slots). Then plant the seedlings out at the correct distances. This means you use far fewer seeds, you don't waste time thinning out the crop, and you give your plants a far better chance of establishing quickly. The technique is vital for late autumn salad leaves.

24

Run out of flower pots? Be bold!

You'll find a huge variety of (usually free) containers to use as planters. Wheelbarrows, porcelain sinks, lavatory bowls, paddling pools, baskets, buckets, old wellingtons, car tyres, even the drum from a washing machine – they all have their uses.

25

Make your own compost,

rather than buying expensive bags from the garden centre. Improvise a bin (with timber or plastic) and fill it with vegetable waste, weeds, torn-up newspaper, ash, soil and any other organic material which breaks down fast. You can speed the process up with human urine (diluted).

26

Save money on chemical pesticides

– by using natural ones. The best bug killers are birds, so attract them to your garden with food. Swot up on companion planting (such as carrots with onions), by which plants deter each others' pests. Scatter coffee grounds or ground eggshell to keep insect nasties at bay.

27

You can **find free garden tools and other equipment**

if you know where to look. The most obvious place is the local household waste or recycling centre (you'd be amazed at what gets chucked out). There are also local websites, such as Freecycle, which advertise all manner of free-to-collector stuff.

28

Take cuttings from your plants – and from your friends' plants.

Learn the simple techniques involved in making cuttings, and you'll have free plants to put in your garden, or to swap. Some simple varieties to start with are valerian, geranium, hydrangea, mint, lavender and honeysuckle.

29

Switch to rechargeable batteries

in radios, cameras and other hardware. They (and the charger) may cost more than conventional to start with, but research shows that after only 5 re-charges you'll be in profit.

30

Get a water meter fitted.

This way, you only pay for the water you use, rather than a fixed sum. It is an especially good money-saving option in small households, which will use less anyway. But a meter also helps in bigger establishments to keep accurate tabs on water consumption.

31

Leave your mobile phone at home whenever possible.

One way and another, mobiles cost a lot – and a huge number of calls are pointless and wasteful. Remove the source of temptation, and use the (much cheaper) landline when you get home.

32

Buy an electricity monitor.

It's a salutary exercise to see in stark figures how much power your household uses. A monitor makes it plain which appliances are the most economic, and which the most wasteful. Some suppliers will give you a free one if you ask.

33

Look after the machines in your home –

they may be working below par and wasting valuable energy. Clean out the filters in your washing machine and dishwasher. Check the bag and filters on your vacuum cleaner. Clear the limescale and other gunge out of the kettle. While you're at it, worm the cat.

34

Turn off standby lights.

Those little red or green lights on TVs and DVD players; those clock displays on radios and cookers; lights on phones and chargers – they add up to a considerable leak of electricity. Turn them off or buy more economic models in the first place.

35

A lot of the heat from a radiator goes straight into the wall – and that may mean an outside wall. Put reflecting material behind the radiator to **bounce the heat back.**

You can get specially made reflectors, or simply use kitchen foil.

36

Turn your appliances down and save energy – and money.

Click the central heating thermostat down a degree or two. Wash your clothes at 30° rather than 40°. Turn the sound down on the TV, radio and CD player. Simmer, don't blast, food. Turn the tumble drier off altogether (and permanently).

37

Avoid extended warranties on electrical goods.

Your consumer rights are already protected by law in case something is faulty. Signing up to a standing order just in case your toaster packs up in two years' time seems bonkers.

38

Use your local library – it's free.

Sounds obvious, but many people never go near one. You can borrow books, CDs, and DVDs. You can log on. You can browse the shelves for specific information even Google won't locate. Or you can just sit and read.

39

Overhaul your regular money payments.

Do you need all those subscriptions to magazines you never read or gyms you never visit? Is there any point in buying lottery tickets every week? The cash may be dribbling out of tiny holes, but it all adds up. Put the money in an ISA instead.

40

Is that car really necessary?

A huge number of households now boast at least two cars. Get rid of one, and you'll save at the very least about £15 a week (not to mention the cost of buying the thing in the first place). This may involve getting used to a different travel routine, but it will be worth it.

41

Buy a bicycle and use it.

For short distances, a bike journey can be quick, convenient – and absolutely free. What's more, cycling keeps you fit and is completely pollution-free.

42

Make sure your

car tyres are inflated to the correct pressure.

Tyres which are too hard or too soft will affect your fuel consumption. They will also wear the rubber out more quickly, meaning you'll have to buy new tyres more frequently.

43

Buy fuel in the morning or in the evening.

Sounds odd, but there's a practical reason. On hot days, the fuel in the station storage tanks expands. So you'll get less of it for your money. Fill up in the cool of the day, and end up with more fuel.

44

Turn off your car engine and save fuel.

This one sounds ridiculously obvious, but it's amazing how many people sit in car parks, traffic jams and other situations with their engines trundling away. When you get half a chance, turn it off and enjoy the quiet.

45

Get rid of excess weight in your vehicle.

Do you really need to carry that box of tools, stack of books, sack of gravel, cache of empty bottles everywhere? Extra baggage can easily add up to the weight of an extra person, and increase your consumption of fuel. Travel as light as possible.

46

Use as high a gear as you can.

The higher the gear, the slower the engine turns over, and the less fuel – on average – you use. With skill you will still be able to maintain much the same sort of speeds, but the fuel gauge won't plummet so fast.

47

Book holidays and travel tickets well in advance.

Many companies (especially cheap airlines and train operators) put a certain number of tickets on sale early, at greatly reduced prices. Keep an eye open for these and plan your holiday accordingly.

48

Conversely,

book your holidays at the last minute.

Tour and cruise operators, in particular, are often desperate to fill up the last remaining vacancies. If you can be brave and hang on, you'll see prices steadily fall. Some operators might even be open for offers.

49

Have a clearout – and make money.

Collect together all the unused, unloved, superfluous or forgotten items in your house, weed out anything that's broken or useless, and sell the rest. eBay and similar sites are straightforward to use and – hey presto – you've got a tidier home.

50

Park your car for free.

Have you ever added up the annual cost of parking a car in a town centre? It will be horrendous. Find an unrestricted spot outside the centre and park there. It means more walking, but you save a lot of money and get fitter at the same time.

William Fortt

William Fortt is a keen environmentalist who delights in minimalizing personal waste and enjoys finding and sharing ways to save and prolong our resources. He has been an author for more than 30 years, with many books to his name, including the Little Book of Green Tips (also Absolute Press).

THE LITTLE BOOK OF
BARBECUE
TIPS
ANDREW LANGLEY

THE LITTLE BOOK OF
BEER
TIPS
ANDREW LANGLEY

THE LITTLE BOOK OF
HERB
TIPS
WILLIAM FORTT
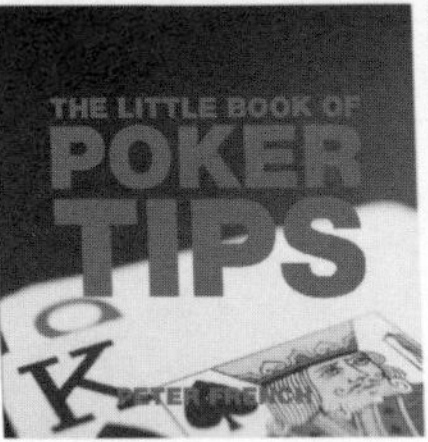
THE LITTLE BOOK OF
POKER
TIPS
PETER FRENCH

THE LITTLE BOOK OF
GARDENING
TIPS
WILLIAM FORTT

THE LITTLE BOOK OF
CHEFS'
TIPS
RICHARD MAGGS

THE LITTLE BOOK OF
SPICE
TIPS
ANDREW LANGLEY
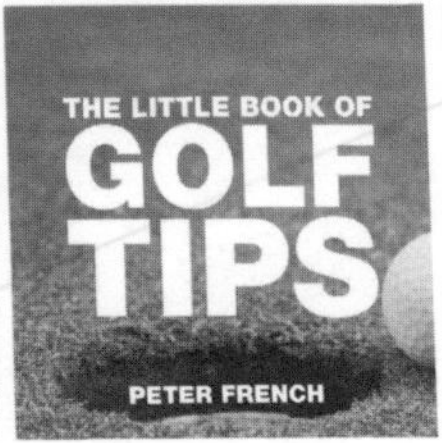
THE LITTLE BOOK OF
GOLF
TIPS
PETER FRENCH

THE LITTLE BOOK OF
TIPS
SERIES

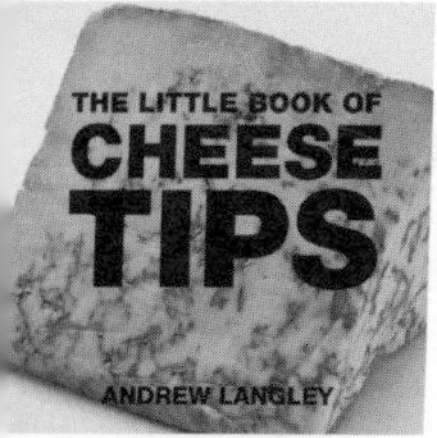
THE LITTLE BOOK OF
CHEESE
TIPS
ANDREW LANGLEY

THE LITTLE BOOK OF
WINE
TIPS
ANDREW LANGLEY

THE LITTLE BOOK OF
AGA
TIPS²
RICHARD MAGGS

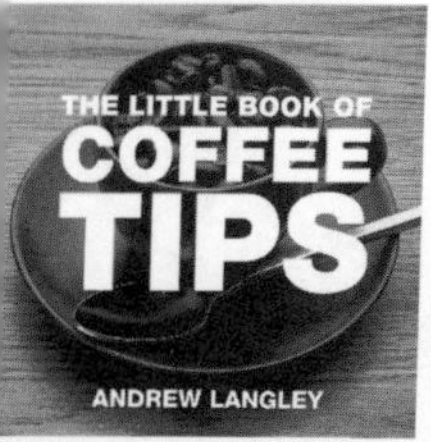
THE LITTLE BOOK OF
COFFEE
TIPS
ANDREW LANGLEY

THE LITTLE BOOK OF
TEA
TIPS
ANDREW LANGLEY

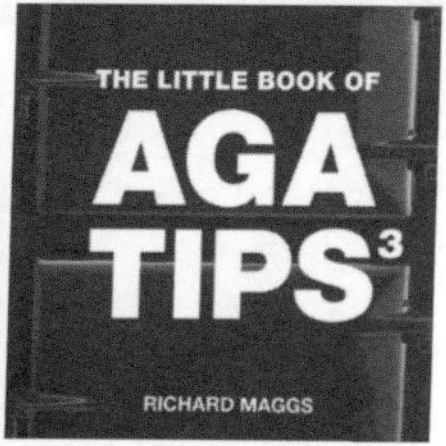
THE LITTLE BOOK OF
AGA
TIPS³
RICHARD MAGGS

THE LITTLE BOOK OF
AGA
TIPS
RICHARD MAGGS

THE LITTLE BOOK OF
CHRISTMAS
AGA
TIPS
RICHARD MAGGS

THE LITTLE BOOK OF
RAYBURN
TIPS
RICHARD MAGGS

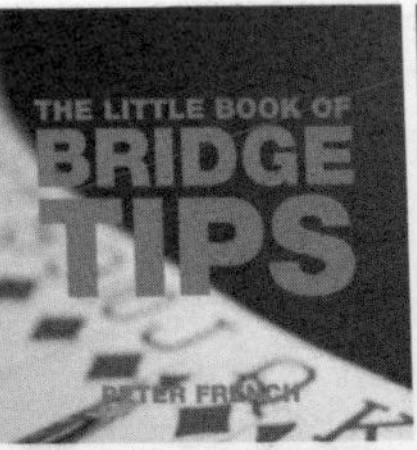
THE LITTLE BOOK OF
BRIDGE
TIPS
PETER FRENCH

THE LITTLE BOOK OF
CHESS
TIPS
PETER FRENCH

THE LITTLE BOOK OF
FISHING
TIPS
MICK DEVENISH

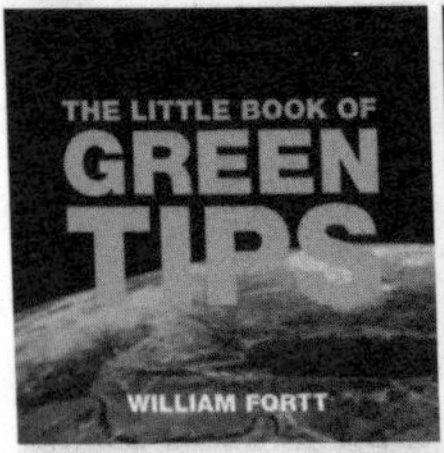
THE LITTLE BOOK OF
GREEN
TIPS
WILLIAM FORTT

THE LITTLE BOOK OF
KITTEN
TIPS
ANDREW LANGLEY

MARMITE
PAUL HARTLEY
THE LITTLE BOOK OF
MARMITE
TIPS

THE LITTLE BOOK OF
PUPPY
TIPS
ANDREW LANGLEY

THE LITTLE BOOK OF
WHISKY
TIPS
ANDREW LANGLEY

THE LITTLE BOOK OF
TRAVEL
TIPS
MEGAN DEVENISH

Little Books of Tips from Absolute Press

Aga Tips
Aga Tips 2
Aga Tips 3
Backgammon Tips
Barbecue Tips
Beer Tips
Bread Tips
Bridge Tips
Cake Decorating Tips
Cheese Tips
Chefs' Tips
Chess Tips
Chocolate Tips
Christmas Aga Tips
Chutney and Pickle Tips
Cocktail Tips
Coffee Tips
Curry Tips
Fishing Tips
Frugal Tips
Gardening Tips
Golf Tips
Green Tips
Grow Your Own Tips
Herb Tips
Houseplant Tips
Jam Tips
Kitten Tips
Macaroon Tips
Marmite Tips
Olive Oil Tips
Pasta Tips
Poker Tips
Puppy Tips
Rayburn Tips
Spice Tips
Tea Tips
Travel Tips
Whisky Tips
Wine Tips
Vinegar Tips